OHIO

Past and Present

Kristi Lew

WITHDRAWN

rosen publishing's
rosen central®

New York

To Peggy and Dave, the coolest Ohioans I know

Published in 2010 by The Rosen Publishing Group, Inc.
29 East 21st Street, New York, NY 10010

First Edition

Library of Congress Cataloging-in-Publication Data

Lew, Kristi.
Ohio: past and present / Kristi Lew.—1st ed.
    p. cm.—(The United States: past and present)
Includes bibliographical references and index.
ISBN-13: 978-1-4358-5286-0 (library binding)
ISBN-13: 978-1-4358-5570-0 (pbk)
ISBN-13: 978-1-4358-5571-7 (6 pack)
1. Ohio—Juvenile literature. I. Title.
F491.3.L49 2010
977.1—dc22

2008054234

Manufactured in the United States of America

On the cover: Top left: In 1803, the Ross County courthouse in Chillicothe became Ohio's first statehouse. Top right: Farming is an important part of Ohio's past, present, and future. Bottom: The Roebling Suspension Bridge in Cincinnati, Ohio.

Contents

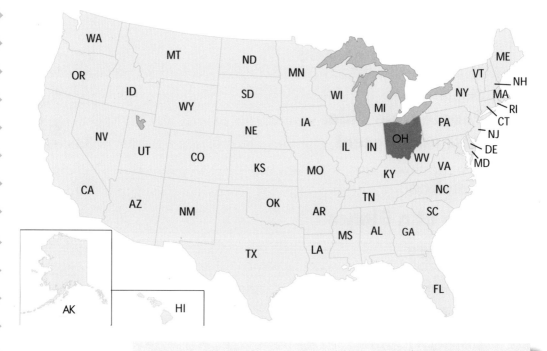

Ohio is the easternmost of the Midwestern states. Lake Erie, one of the Great Lakes, makes up a large portion of Ohio's northern border.

Introduction

Ohioans—natives of Ohio—have had a lasting effect on the history of the United States. Thomas Edison, Harriet Beecher Stowe, and Pete Rose are just a few of the famous people who have called Ohio home. In addition, eight U.S. presidents were born or raised in Ohio, more than in any other state. This has earned Ohio the nickname of the Mother of Presidents.

Ohio is also called the Buckeye State because the land was once covered with buckeye trees. The markings on the nut of the buckeye tree look like the eye of a male deer, or buck. Because of this nickname, people who live in Ohio are sometimes called Buckeyes. Ohio's government has even made the Ohio buckeye the state's official tree.

Ohio is the only state in the country to have an official state rock song, "Hang on Sloopy." The song is about Dorothy Sloop, a singer from Steubenville, Ohio, who sometimes used the stage name Sloopy. In 1965, the song turned into a major hit for a band from Dayton, Ohio, called the McCoys. Later, the band of Ohio State University began playing the song at football games, and in 1985, the Ohio General Assembly made it the official rock song of the state.

It is rather fitting that the only state to have an official state rock song is also home to the Rock and Roll Hall of Fame. The 150,000-square-foot (almost 14,000 square meters) museum opened in September 1995 in downtown Cleveland. It has attracted more than seven million visitors interested in learning about the history of rock and roll.

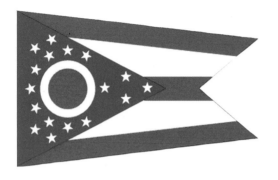

The Ohio Burgee has the swallow-tailed shape of many flags flown on ships or yachts.

Ohioans seem to be partial to the color red. The official state beverage, tomato juice, is red. So are the state bird (the cardinal), the state flower (the red carnation), and the state insect (the ladybug).

Even Ohio's state flag, adopted in 1902, has red on it. Like the national flag, Ohio's state flag sports the colors red, white, and blue. Seventeen white stars, representing the fact that Ohio was the seventeenth state to join the Union, sit on a blue triangular background. This section of the flag also contains a large white circle with a smaller red circle inside of it. These circles represent the letter "O" in Ohio. The circles also look like the pattern on the buckeye nut that gives the state its popular nickname.

Ohio's state quarter, part of the U.S. Mint's 50 State Quarters Program, calls the state the Birthplace of Aviation Pioneers. Orville and Wilbur Wright (the inventors of the airplane), John Glenn (the first American to orbit Earth), and Neil Armstrong (the first American to walk on the moon) were all born or raised in Ohio.

Chapter 1

THE LAND OF
OHIO

Ohio is a state in the Midwest region, or central part, of the United States. Along with Ohio, the Midwestern states include Michigan, Indiana, Illinois, Wisconsin, Missouri, Minnesota, Iowa, Kansas, North Dakota, South Dakota, and Nebraska. Ohio is the easternmost of these states.

With a land area of about 41,000 square miles (about 106,190 square km), Ohio is the thirty-fourth largest state in the country. The state measures over 200 miles (322 km) from east to west and from north to south. Ohio lies between Indiana to the west and Pennsylvania to the east. Lake Erie makes up a portion of Ohio's northern border, and Michigan makes up the rest. Kentucky is to Ohio's south, and West Virginia lies to the southeast.

Because of its location, Ohio experiences all four seasons: fall, winter, spring, and summer. Summers can be very hot and humid. In fact, the highest temperature ever recorded in Ohio was 113 degrees Fahrenheit (45 degrees Celsius), near Gallipolis in July 1934. The winters in Ohio can be brutally cold. The coldest temperature ever measured with modern instruments in Ohio, -39°F (-39.4°C), was recorded in February 1899 in Milligan. While this temperature is cold, this is not the coldest that Ohio has ever been.

Ice Age Ohio

Between 1.8 million and 14,000 years ago, much of present-day Ohio's land was covered in layers and layers of slowly moving ice. Large ice sheets like these are called glaciers. At their peak, the glaciers were nearly a mile (1.6 km) thick where Lake Erie lies today. In central Ohio, they were almost 1,000 feet (about 305 m) thick. This ice covered almost two-thirds of the state.

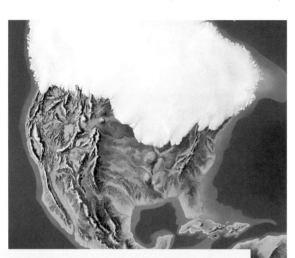

Glaciers covered almost two-thirds of Ohio during the last ice age. Most of Ohio's landforms were created by these ice sheets.

Most of the landforms now present in Ohio are made up of sand, gravel, and soil that were moved and deposited by glaciers. As glaciers move across the land, the ice picks up rocks and soil. The rocks and soil are carried away when the ice moves, and they are deposited in other places when the ice melts. Glaciers also push soil as they move, and they erode, or wear away, the rocks beneath them. During the process of erosion, the glaciers break up the rock into small pieces. Glaciers with rocks embedded in them can carve deep grooves into the land's surface. You can see an example of the scratches made by Ohio's glaciers on Kelleys Island in Lake Erie.

Lake Erie

About seventy thousand years ago, the last of the glaciers that would march across Ohio started to form. Called the Wisconsinan glacier, this enormous ice sheet covered almost all of Canada and dipped down into the United States. This glacier flattened mountains and dug deep valleys as it advanced across the landscape, eroding the underlying bedrock. When the glacier started to melt and retreat around fourteen thousand years ago, it left behind ridges, glacial deposits, and lots of meltwater. The water poured into the valleys created by the glacier, forming the Great Lakes—including Lake Erie.

Today, the 312 miles (502 km) of Lake Erie's shoreline in Ohio are dotted with dozens of towns, including Cleveland, Toledo, and Sandusky. Ohio farmers and manufacturers use the lake's natural waterways and man-made canals to transport their products. More than 100 million tons of goods, from rock salt and coal to grain and stone, travel through Lake Erie's ports each year. But not all Ohioans use the lake for transportation and commerce. Many people just like to take advantage of the lake's beauty on their vacations.

Ohio's Natural Regions

The geography of Ohio was determined by prehistoric ice. The areas that were once covered by glaciers are quite different from the areas that were not scoured by the gigantic ice sheets.

Ohio can be split up into several different geographic regions: the Lake Plains region, the Till Plains region, the Appalachian Plateaus, and the Interior Low Plateau (sometimes referred to as the Bluegrass region or the Lexington Plain). These regions are defined by the

GEOGRAPHIC REGIONS OF OHIO

Lake Plains

Glaciated Appalachian Plateau

Till Plains

Unglaciated Appalachian Plateau

Interior Low Plateau Bluegrass Section

Ohio has five main regions. Each region is defined by the type of soil and landforms it contains.

landforms and soil present in each of them.

The Lake Plains region lies along the southern shores of Lake Erie in the northwestern part of the state. It is a flat region that was formed by ancient lakes. The Great Black Swamp is a part of this region. Before the state was settled, the swamp was a dense forest that flooded much of the year. Ohioans drained the swamp in the nineteenth century, and the area now has some of the most fertile soil in the country.

Most of western Ohio is part of the Till Plains region. Till is a kind of soil made up of clay, silt, and rocks. Glaciers deposited the till as they moved across the area. The soil in this region is very fertile and well suited to farming. Campbell Hill, the highest point in Ohio, was formed by material that was built up by glaciers. The lowest part of Ohio is also in this region, along the course of the Ohio River near Cincinnati.

The Appalachian Plateau is broken up into two regions based on whether or not the area was once covered by glaciers. The Glaciated Appalachian Plateau begins in the northeastern part of the state and

The Ohio River forms the state's southern border, separating it from Kentucky and West Virginia. Cincinnati lies on the northern banks of the Ohio River in the Till Plains region.

stretches in a band toward the middle. Because glaciers once covered this area and flattened the land, it has wide, flat valleys and gently rolling hills. This region is good for farming. The Unglaciated Appalachian Plateau lies to the south of this area. Because heavy sheets of ice never flattened this region, it has more rugged hills than the glaciated plateau. This area also tends to have poor soil, so it is not usually farmed. Instead, it is covered with forests.

The Interior Low Plateau—also known as the Bluegrass region or Lexington Plain—is a small triangular region located along Ohio's southwestern border. It reaches up into Ohio's Adams County from Kentucky and is known for its rolling hills. The name "Bluegrass" comes from a type of grass that grows easily in the area.

Including Lake Erie, Ohio has more than 2,500 lakes and more than 44,000 miles (70,811 km) of rivers and streams. One of the lakes, Grand Lake, is the largest man-made lake in the world built without machinery. Between 1837 and 1845, 1,700 men worked with hand tools to construct the lake. Major rivers in the state include the Ohio, Miami, Cuyahoga, Maumee, Muskingham, Scioto, and Sandusky rivers.

Animal and Plant Life in Ohio

More than sixty species of mammals live in Ohio, including foxes, raccoons, skunks, rabbits, and muskrats. The white-tailed deer— Ohio's state mammal—is one of the largest. Many birds, reptiles, and fish also call the state home. Including the cardinal, Ohio's state bird, 350 bird species can be found statewide. The state's official reptile is the black racer, a fast-moving snake. The state is home to forty-six other reptile species, including many types of turtles and lizards. Ohio's abundant streams, lakes, and rivers house many types of fish. Bass, perch, trout, pike, drum, and catfish can all be found in Ohio's waterways.

At one time, 95 percent of Ohio was covered by hardwood forests. Today, less than 30 percent of these forests remain, mainly in southern and eastern Ohio. The most common trees in these hardwood forests are oaks, maples, and hickories. Beech, black walnut, and Virginia pine trees can also be found. Several small flowering trees and shrubs, including magnolias, dogwoods, and honeysuckle, are abundant. The state's wildflowers include the black-eyed Susan, goldenrod, sunflower, aster, thistle, and Queen Anne's lace.

Chapter 2

THE HISTORY OF OHIO

People lived in the area of Ohio long before written records were kept. Social scientists call people who lived before written history prehistoric. Prehistoric people arrived in Ohio 9,500 years ago or more, after the glaciers retreated. Scientists know this because the people left behind artifacts, or objects that they made and used.

The First Ohioans: Prehistoric People

The first Ohioans lived in the region prior to 8000 BCE. Scientists call this group of people the Paleo-Indians. The Paleo-Indians were hunters. They hunted large animals like mastodons and mammoths, which are now extinct, as well as smaller animals like deer and birds. The Paleo-Indians used spear points made from flint, a stone that was abundant in Ohio. Some of these spear points can still be found in Ohio today.

When the climate warmed, thick forests grew. Large mammals, such as mammoths and mastodons, died out. This forced people to rely on smaller animals like bison, deer, bears, wild turkey, and elk for food. Scientists call the people who lived in Ohio from 8000 to 500 BCE the Archaic people. Like their ancestors the Paleo-Indians, the Archaic people used flint to make spear points. They also used other stones to make tools, such as granite for axes. They used the axes to chop down trees and form dugout canoes.

The Woodland Period

Archaeologists call the period from about 800 BCE to 1200 CE the Woodland period. The way people lived during this period was different. Instead of always moving from place to place, they settled down and lived in villages. They also farmed using local plants, including sunflowers and squash. They started to make and use ceramic pottery.

The Miamisburg Mound in Montgomery County is the largest surviving mound built by the Adena people. At one time, the mound was more than 70 feet (21.3 m) high.

The Adena people lived in eastern Ohio during this time period. The Adena people built mounds of earth for ceremonial purposes, for places to gather, and for places to bury their dead. The largest surviving mound of the Adena people is the Miamisburg Mound in Montgomery County.

The Hopewell people also lived during the Woodland period, in southern and central Ohio. Their culture developed from the Adena culture. The Hopewell people also built elaborate earth mounds near Chillicothe and Newark. The Newark Earthworks, Ohio's official state prehistoric monument, is the largest geometric mound left behind by the Hopewell people.

Frontier Ohio

From the end of the Woodland period until just before the Europeans arrived (900 to 1650 CE), many Native American tribes flourished in Ohio. Here, they grew maize, squash, and beans to feed their families. They also hunted and fished.

By 1650, the powerful Iroquois began to take over Ohio. They fought and pushed out the other Native American groups. In fact, the Iroquois gave Ohio its name, which means "great river." Later, as the Iroquois became less powerful, groups such as the Delaware, the Shawnee, the Miami, and the Ottawa joined them in Ohio.

These Native Americans thrived until French explorers discovered the area. Nicholas Sanson made the earliest map of northern Ohio in 1650. Sanson's map showed the large lake that eventually would be called Lake Erie, as well as the many rivers flowing southward from the lake.

In 1669, René-Robert Cavelier Sieur de La Salle, a French explorer, arrived in the Ohio Valley. He was the first European to see the Ohio

River. La Salle quickly claimed the entire Ohio Valley for France. Fur traders and people from the East seeking new farmland were soon attracted to the area.

The French may have been the first Europeans to reach Ohio, but the British were not far behind. Challenging the French, the British also claimed the land known as Ohio Country. Struggles for control between the French and the British eventually erupted into the French and Indian War. From 1754 to 1763, Native Americans fought alongside the French, with whom they were friendly. However, they were no match for the British army. When the British won the conflict, the French were driven from Ohio Country.

According to the treaty signed in 1763, the French lands now belonged to the British. The British took over the French forts and began to build new forts and settlements. The Native Americans feared a flood of new settlers, and under the leadership of an Ottawa chief named Pontiac, they decided to mount a rebellion. The Ottawas attacked Fort Detroit in May 1763. Other Native American groups began to raid British settlements.

Hoping to avoid more struggles with the Native Americans, the British passed the Proclamation of 1763, which made it illegal for colonists to live west of the Appalachian Mountains. This area was set aside for the Native Americans. The law improved relations between the Native Americans and England, but the colonists were upset. They wanted to settle in Ohio Country.

Hoping to keep the law in place, many Native American tribes decided to fight on the side of the British during the American Revolutionary War. However, the American colonists defeated the British, allowing settlers to move west freely.

Ohio Becomes a State

In 1787, the Confederation Congress (the first legislature of the new United States) passed the Northwest Ordinance. This act created the Northwest Territory out of the land east of the Mississippi and west of Pennsylvania between the Ohio River and the Great Lakes. It required that the territory be broken up into at least three states, but no more than five.

In 1788, the Ohio Company of Associates, which was established to settle the land around the Ohio River, sent a forty-eight-member expedition team to found the city of Marietta. Many of the first settlers came from New England. Once they were established, they set about creating communities similar to the ones they had left behind.

One of the first maps of the new state of Ohio was made by Rufus Putnam in 1803.

Settlers moving into the Northwest Territory struggled with the Native Americans for control of the land. President George Washington appointed General Anthony Wayne to command the army in the area in order to protect settlers from Native American attacks. In 1794, Wayne and his troops fought a ferocious battle against the Native Americans, who were led by Blue Jacket. It was called the Battle of the Fallen Timbers because the Native Americans used trees uprooted by a tornado as cover. The Native Americans lost badly. The next year, they signed the Treaty of Greeneville, in which they agreed to move to the northwestern part of Ohio. This left the lands to the south and east to the settlers.

Ohio native General Ulysses S. Grant led the victorious Union troops in the U.S. Civil War.

In 1802, the Ohio territory began the process of becoming a state. On February 19, 1803, Ohio became the first state formed from the Northwest Territory and the seventeenth state of the United States.

By 1860, Ohioans built canals, highways, and railroads to connect them with other states. They also built factories, which produced goods to sell to those states. Ohio grew from 45,365 residents in 1800 to more than 2.3 million people in 1860. At that point, Ohio was a thriving state.

The Civil War

From 1861 to 1865, the American Civil War raged between the Northern states, which believed slaves should be freed, and the

Southern states, which did not. Many Ohioans sought to help African American slaves escape the South. Through the Underground Railroad, a system of safe houses and other hiding places, thousands of runaway slaves passed through Ohio.

Only two Civil War battles took place in Ohio: one near Buffington Island and the other at Salineville. Nevertheless, Ohioans played a major role in this conflict. More than three hundred thousand Ohioans fought in the war, including the generals George McClellan, William Tecumseh Sherman, and Ulysses S. Grant. Grant later became president of the United States. So did three other Civil War veterans from Ohio: Rutherford B. Hayes, James Garfield, and William McKinley.

Ohio Grows, Changes, and Fights

Between 1860 and the early 1920s, much of Ohio's population moved from rural farming communities to large cities, where people worked in factories or offices. As new employees moved into the state to keep businesses running, Ohio's population again grew by almost two million people.

The job outlook in Ohio changed when the Great Depression hit the country in the early 1930s. Forty percent of Ohio's factory workers and 67 percent of its construction

By the mid-1900s, many Ohioans worked in factories like the United States Steel Corporation in Youngstown.

Camp Sherman

In July 1917, construction of Camp Sherman (named for the Civil War general William Tecumseh Sherman) began on 2,000 acres (809 hectares) of land near Chillicothe. Camp Sherman was the third-largest training camp for U.S. troops during World War I. More than forty-thousand soldiers passed through Camp Sherman by the time the war ended. The camp, which was built on the site of Hopewell mounds, consisted of 1,370 buildings. It had two movie theaters, a laundry, a library, a hospital, and a prison that held German prisoners of war. The camp also had its own working farm, complete with vegetable gardens and dairy cows. World War I ended in November 1918, and Camp Sherman was closed in the 1920s.

Today, nothing is left of the original Camp Sherman. All of the buildings were demolished by the U.S. government. However, the land where the camp once stood is now the site of the Veterans Administration Medical Center, the Ross Correctional Institution, the Hopewell Culture National Historical Park, the Chillicothe Correctional Institution, and a wildlife refuge.

Camp Sherman was a large training camp for U.S. troops during World War I.

workers lost their jobs. Many people were forced to move away from Ohio's cities and return to farming to feed their families.

The beginning of World War II ended the Great Depression in the 1940s. Ohio sent many of its citizens to fight in the war. The war ended on August 6, 1945, when the United States dropped two atomic bombs on Japan. Ohio scientists at the Battelle Memorial Institute in Columbus were instrumental in developing these bombs. The *Enola Gay*, the plane that carried the bomb dropped on Hiroshima, was flown by Ohioan Paul Tibbets.

Events in Ohio had a profound effect on the way the U.S. government handled another conflict—the Vietnam War. Beginning in the late 1950s, the United States became involved in a conflict between Communist North Vietnam and South Vietnam. It was a very bloody conflict in which more than fifty thousand Americans were killed and at least one hundred and fifty thousand more were wounded.

Many Americans protested the Vietnam conflict, including some students at Kent State University in Ohio. In May 1970, Ohio's National Guard was called in to make sure the protests did not get out of hand. They tried to subdue the protesters with tear gas. In response, some of the protesters threw rocks and bottles at the soldiers. Eventually, the tension between the two groups boiled over and the soldiers fired their weapons into the crowed, killing four Kent State students and wounding nine others.

After the Kent State riots, protests against the involvement of U.S. troops in the Vietnam War increased dramatically in other parts of the country. Three years later, President Richard Nixon signed the Paris Peace Accords and U.S. soldiers started to leave Vietnam.

Present-Day Ohio

Today, Ohio is the seventh most populous state in America. Nearly three million people live in the Cleveland, Akron, and Elyria area, making it Ohio's largest metropolitan area. Other large cities with at

Today, Ohio is a thriving state with bustling cities like Cleveland. The Rock and Roll Hall of Fame and Museum *(at left)* is a Cleveland landmark.

least half a million people include Cincinnati, Columbus, Dayton, Toledo, and Youngstown.

The population and job market in Ohio continue to change. From 1976 until today, Ohio has struggled with closing businesses and factories. Many workers have lost their jobs. The closing of the factories where many people worked has caused Ohio's economy to shift. Today, there are more opportunities in service jobs than in industry and manufacturing. Ohioans are working hard to bring new businesses to the state and to revitalize their towns and cities.

Chapter 3

THE GOVERNMENT OF OHIO

According to Ohio's state constitution, the state government consists of three branches: a legislative branch, an executive branch, and a judicial branch. The branches of Ohio's government work together to pass, enforce, change, and remove laws for the benefit of all Ohioans.

Making Laws

The legislative branch of Ohio's government includes the House of Representatives and the Senate. The House of Representatives is composed of ninety-nine members with two-year terms. The Senate is made up of thirty-three members with four-year terms. Together, these two bodies are called the Ohio General Assembly.

When legislators write a new law, they first create a draft of the law called a bill. This draft can be changed as needed. Bills are read, changed, and voted on by both the House and the Senate. If a majority of the assembly members think the bill should be turned into a law, the bill becomes an act and it is sent to the governor's office. If the governor agrees that the law is a good idea, he or she signs it and the act becomes a state law.

However, the governor also has the power to reject, or veto, the bill. A vetoed bill goes back to the General Assembly. The General

In 1816, the state capital was moved from Chillicothe to Columbus. Construction of the Ohio Statehouse began in 1839. The building was completed twenty-two years later.

Assembly members may decide to change the bill, vote on it again, and send it back to the governor to sign. Or they may decide the bill should become a law as written. If this happens, they can override the governor's veto as long as three-fifths of the representatives and senators vote to do so.

Enforcing Laws

The executive branch of government makes sure that laws are enforced. The governor is the head of the executive branch. He or

The State Capital

In 1812, the Ohio legislature decided the growing state needed to find a central location for its capital city. The state government had already tried using several locations, including Chillicothe and Zanesville, but these were not satisfactory. The state government chose a spot on the eastern bank of the Scioto River, where there was not yet a town. The building of the city of Columbus, named for the explorer Christopher Columbus, began that year. By 1813, the first church, school, jail, and newspaper had been established. In 1816, the town was named Ohio's state capital.

Today, Columbus is still the seat of Ohio's government. Columbus has a thriving economic and cultural life. The headquarters of several large companies, such as Nationwide Insurance, American Electric Power, Limited Brands, Big Lots, and Bob Evans Farms, make their home in the city. When the city's residents are not working, the Columbus Museum of Art, the Ohio Historical Society, the Center for Ohio Science and Industry, and the Columbus Zoo and Aquarium are just a few of the resources available to entertain and educate them.

she is responsible for signing into law or vetoing bills passed by the legislature. The governor also proposes a state budget and appoints members of the various state boards and commissions. He or she also appoints directors of state departments, such as the Department of Agriculture, the Department of Public Safety, the Environmental Protection Agency, and many others.

Other members of the executive branch include the lieutenant governor, attorney general, auditor of state, secretary of state, treasurer of state, and state board of education. Ohio's executive branch members are elected to serve four-year terms.

The ninety-nine members of the Ohio House of Representatives meet in the House Chambers of the Ohio Statehouse.

Interpreting the Laws

Even though the legislative branch is very careful when it writes laws, it cannot predict all of the ways in which they may be applied. Ohio's judicial branch ensures that laws are interpreted the way the legislative branch intended. All of the state's courts are part of the judicial branch.

When a law is broken in Ohio, the case is first heard in one of the state's lower courts. These include the municipal courts, the county courts, and the courts of common pleas. If all parties are not satisfied with the decision made by a court, then an appeal can be filed. Appeals are heard by one of Ohio's twelve district courts of appeal. If a defendant is not content with the decision of the court of appeals, then the defendant may appeal to Ohio's highest court: the Supreme Court of Ohio. That court's decision on a case is final.

Ohio's supreme court has seven judges. When a case appears before the court, the judges listen to both sides of the case and then vote to decide what should be done. At least four of the justices must vote the same way for the case to be decided. The court's interpretation of the law is published, and the decision becomes the law of the state. The justices are elected by the citizens of Ohio to serve eight-year terms.

Local Government

Each of Ohio's eighty-eight counties has its own local government. Every four years, a three-member board of commissioners is elected by the citizens of each county. The board of commissioners is responsible for creating the county's budget and sticking to it. They also decide how land in the county will be used, and they determine other general policies for the county as well. To help the board of commissioners fulfill their duties, citizens elect a county financial officer, clerk of courts, coroner, engineer, prosecuting attorney, recorder, sheriff, and treasurer.

Within each of Ohio's counties there are villages, townships, and cities. There are many different ways these municipalities can be governed, but most elect a mayor and council members. The mayor is the highest elected official and is responsible for the budget and public safety. The town or city council acts as a legislative branch and decides on overall policies for the town.

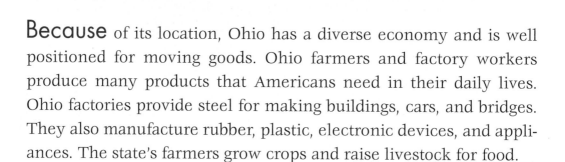

THE ECONOMY OF OHIO

Because of its location, Ohio has a diverse economy and is well positioned for moving goods. Ohio farmers and factory workers produce many products that Americans need in their daily lives. Ohio factories provide steel for making buildings, cars, and bridges. They also manufacture rubber, plastic, electronic devices, and appliances. The state's farmers grow crops and raise livestock for food.

Agriculture

The two top crops in Ohio are soybeans and corn. Other vegetables grown by Ohio farmers include cucumbers, potatoes, and tomatoes, as well as smaller amounts of cabbage, celery, lettuce, peppers, and snap beans. Fruits, including apples, grapes, peaches, and strawberries, also thrive in the region. Wheat, hay, and oats for feeding livestock, as well as greenhouse and nursery plants, are grown in Ohio, too.

Farmers in Ohio raise livestock, such as dairy cows, chickens, and hogs. The dairy cows produce the leading livestock product in Ohio: milk. Ohio ranks first in the nation in the production of Swiss cheese. It's also the second-largest provider of eggs in the United States.

Ohio pioneers even produced their own breed of hog, called the Poland China hog. They bred different kinds of hogs to produce this

Chapter 4

prized, hearty specimen. Ohio farmers also raise turkeys, beef cattle, and sheep. The sheep are raised for their meat as well as their wool. In fact, Ohio is the largest producer of wool east of the Mississippi River.

Corn is one of Ohio's largest crops. Harvested corn is transported to grain elevators. The grain is dumped into bins and raised to the silos for storage.

Manufacturing

Manufacturing is the process of making useful products from raw materials. In Ohio, manufacturing is a leading economic activity because of the state's many factories and plants.

Making car parts and assembling motor vehicles is a large part of Ohio's economy. Honda, General Motors, Ford, and DaimlerChrysler all have plants in Ohio. Other companies, including the Goodyear Corporation, process and manufacture tires and other rubber products for cars.

Ohio is a leading producer of steel. AK Steel, ArcelorMittal, and Wheeling-Pittsburgh Steel are steel manufacturing plants located in the state. Manufacturing plants in Ohio make tools, hardware, and pipe fittings from steel.

Processing chemicals—like chlorine, sodium, calcium, and magnesium, which have many different applications—is the third-largest industry in the state. Sherwin Williams, a large paint and varnish company, is located in Ohio. Other large companies that call Ohio home include Proctor & Gamble and Smuckers.

Mining

Many Ohioans are employed by companies that assemble cars, trucks, and motorcycles.

Another large sector of Ohio's economy is mining. Coal, natural gas, sandstone, lime, and clay are all mined in the state. These natural resources are used to produce electricity. Both sandstone and lime are used in the building industry. Lime is also useful in making cement, chemicals, fertilizer, and steel. Ohio is the top producer of clay in the United States. Clay is used to make cement, tiles, bricks, and pottery.

The first natural resource mined in Ohio was salt. In the 1800s, when settlers were drilling for natural gas, they discovered large salt deposits outside of what is now Cleveland. Millions of years ago, a shallow, salty sea covered eastern Ohio. When the sea evaporated, layers and layers of the mineral were left behind. Today, Ohio mines almost four million tons of salt a year, making it one of the top producers in the country.

Higher Education and Research

Education is very important to Ohioans. The state is home to fifteen public universities, seventy-one private colleges, and twenty-four technical and community colleges. Not only do these institutions of higher learning employ professors, librarians, and janitors, among

Farming in Ohio

Before the 1800s, most Ohioans were farmers. Native Americans in Ohio grew corn, beans, squash, yams, onions, turnips, cabbage, and pumpkins. When Europeans introduced watermelon and muskmelon in the 1700s, Native Ohioans started to grow these as well. Most of the pioneers that settled Ohio were farmers, too. They mainly raised wheat, corn, and other grains. By 1849, Ohio farmers were the leading corn producers in the United States and were second in wheat production.

In the second half of the twentieth century, the prices of agricultural goods dropped and the cost of living went up. This drove most Ohioans to the cities and suburbs, where they could get higher-paying jobs in manufacturing. Today, less than 3 percent of Ohio's citizens own a family farm. However, the average size of farms has increased, and almost half of the land in Ohio is still used for farming.

Ohio farmers grow crops and raise livestock, including dairy cows, chickens, hogs, and sheep.

others, they also prepare students to work in Ohio and other parts of the country.

These institutions do important research. Ohio State University, Case Western Reserve University, and the University of Cincinnati are major research institutions as well as schools. The Cleveland Clinic, a teaching and research hospital, is rated as one of America's top medical centers. Research is also carried out at the National Aeronautics

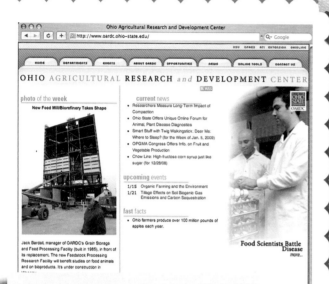

Ohio's scientists hope to improve the lives of people around the world with their research efforts.

and Space Administration's Glenn Research Center and the Battelle Memorial Institute, a science and technical research center. In addition, a number of private companies have research centers related to industry. Altogether, about $8.6 billion is spent in Ohio on research to gain knowledge and make new products and technology.

Service

Some of Ohio's industries, such as farming and manu-facturing, are struggling as jobs shift to other states or countries. However, experts believe that the service industry will see an increase in jobs through at least 2014. The service industry includes businesses like retail stores, restaurants, hotels, repair shops, and engineering and law firms. Jobs in this industry include store clerks, waiters, chefs, bartenders, mechanics, customer service representa-tives, engineers, and lawyers.

Chapter 5

PEOPLE FROM OHIO:
PAST AND PRESENT

Just as Ohio has many diverse industries, it's also a land of diverse and talented people. Prominent American aviators, astronauts, and inventors have come from Ohio. Eight American presidents have called Ohio home. Many of the country's most famous artists, writers, directors, and actors hail from the state as well.

Neil Armstrong (1930–) Neil Armstrong, the first person to walk on the moon, was born in Wapakoneta. He was a U.S. Navy pilot during the Korean War, flying seventy-eight combat missions. He became an astronaut in 1962 and was part of the first manned lunar mission in 1969. Armstrong left the National Aeronautics and Space Administration (NASA) in 1971 and took a position in the aerospace engineering department of the University of Cincinnati.

Drew Carey (1958–) Comedian Drew Carey is from Cleveland, Ohio. His hit television show, *The Drew Carey Show*, was even set in Cleveland. The show's theme song was called "Cleveland Rocks."

Thomas Alva Edison (1847–1931) Thomas Edison, inventor of the incandescent lightbulb, the phonograph, and the motion picture camera, was born in Milan, Ohio, in 1847. Some of his family members have restored the three-story brick home in which the great inventor was born.

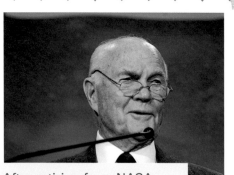

After retiring from NASA, John Glenn became a U.S. senator for Ohio. He served in the Senate until 1999.

John H. Glenn Jr. (1921–) John H. Glenn Jr. was born in Cambridge, Ohio. Glenn was one of the first seven astronauts at NASA. In 1962, John Glenn became the first American to orbit Earth.

Virginia Hamilton (1936–2002) Virginia Hamilton wrote or edited more than thirty children's books. Hamilton grew up on a small farm near Yellow Springs, Ohio. Her writing won many major prizes, including the National Book Award, the John Newbery Medal, and the Hans Christian Andersen Medal.

Toni Morrison (1931–) Toni Morrison was born Chloe Anthony Wofford in Lorain, Ohio. In 1993, Morrison became the first African American woman to be awarded the Nobel Prize in Literature. Her novels include *The Bluest Eye*, *Song of Solomon*, and *Beloved*.

Jack Nicklaus (1940–)

Jack Nicklaus, a professional golfer, was born in Columbus. Over the course of his career, he won one hundred major golf tournaments, including four U.S. Opens, three British Opens, five PGA championships, and six Masters titles.

Toni Morrison has won many literary prizes including the Nobel Prize in Literature and the Pulitzer Prize.

Annie Oakley (1860–1926)

Born in a log cabin on the Ohio frontier, Phoebe Ann Mozee adopted the stage name Annie Oakley when she became an entertainer and sharpshooter in Buffalo Bill's Wild West show. Oakley started hunting animals to support her family at the age of nine. By the time she was sixteen, she was entering and winning shooting contests. She joined Buffalo Bill's show when she was twenty-five and stayed with the show for seventeen years.

Jesse Owens (1913–1980)

Jesse Owens won four gold medals in track and field at the 1936 Olympic Games in Berlin, Germany. Owens moved to Cleveland when he was eight years old. He got his start on his Cleveland high school's track team, and he broke many records as an athlete at Ohio State University.

Ohio and the Automotive Industry

During the late 1800s and early 1900s, several Ohioans played an important part in the fledgling automotive industry. John William Lambert of Ohio City built the first automobile that ran on gasoline. Garrett Morgan developed the first stoplight after witnessing an accident while living in Cleveland. Charles Kettering of General Motors invented electric ignitions; in the past, drivers had to turn a hand crank to get their cars started. Kettering also invented sparkplugs, electric headlights, and the automatic transmission.

Today, Ohio is ranked second in automobile production. Ohioans working in automotive plants assemble 1.7 million vehicles a year and bring $20 million into the state's economy. Ohio ranks first in the number of auto suppliers—businesses that provide engines, wheels, and other parts. Many of the major automotive companies, including Ford Motor Company, General Motors, Honda, Toyota, and Mitsubishi, either maintain large manufacturing plants there or are headquartered in the state.

Roy Plunkett (1910–1994) In 1938, Roy Plunkett of New Carlisle, Ohio, accidentally invented Teflon while working for DuPont. He also helped develop Freon, a safe, effective coolant to use in refrigerators.

Judith Resnick (1949–1986) Born and raised in Akron, Judith Resnick was the second American woman in space after Sally Ride. After completing her college and graduate education, Resnick was chosen to enter astronaut training in 1978. She flew her first mission for NASA in 1984. She died when the space shuttle *Challenger* exploded on January 28, 1986.

James Murray Spangler (1848–1915) James Murray Spangler got the idea for the electric vacuum cleaner in 1907 while working as a janitor in Canton, Ohio. He started a company to make and sell his machines, but he didn't have much success until his cousin-in-law, William Hoover, took over the company. In time, the Hoover Company became the most famous vacuum cleaner maker in the world.

Robert Lawrence (R. L.) Stine (1943–) R. L. Stine, the author of the Goosebumps book series, was born in Columbus. So far, he has written more than two hundred horror books to scare the pants off of young adult readers.

Harriet Beecher Stowe (1811–1896) Harriet Beecher Stowe's family moved to Cincinnati when she was twenty-one years old. While living in Ohio, Stowe met some of the conductors of the Underground Railroad and the runaway slaves they were helping. This inspired her to write *Uncle Tom's Cabin*, a novel about slavery.

Orville Wright (1871–1948) and Wilbur Wright (1867–1912) The Wright brothers, inventors of the first mechanically powered airplane, grew up in Dayton. They successfully demonstrated their airplane at Kitty Hawk, North Carolina, on December 17, 1903. They proved that powered flight was possible.

Orville and Wilbur Wright invented, built, and flew the first successful mechanically powered airplane.

Timeline

1650	First map of the Ohio region is made by Nicholas Sanson.
1754	French and Indian War begins.
1763	France surrenders the Ohio region to Britain.
1783	Confederation Congress forms the Northwest Territory.
1803	Ohio becomes the seventeenth state of the United States.
1840	William Henry Harrison is elected president.
1843	Last Native Americans are forced off their reservation and relocated to Kansas.
1851	The Ohio constitution is adopted.
1868	Ulysses S. Grant is elected president.
1876	Rutherford B. Hayes is elected president.
1879	Cleveland becomes the first city with electric lights.
1880	James Garfield is elected president.
1888	Benjamin Harrison is elected president.
1897	William McKinley is elected president.
1902	Current Ohio flag is adopted.
1908	William Howard Taft is elected president.
1920	Warren G. Harding is elected president.
1936	Jesse Owens wins four Olympic gold metals in the Berlin games.
1962	John Glenn becomes the first American to orbit Earth.
1969	Neil Armstrong becomes the first man to walk on the moon.
1970	Four Kent State students are shot and killed during Vietnam War protests.
1995	Rock and Roll Hall of Fame and Museum opens in Cleveland.
1998	John Glenn, age seventy-seven, becomes the oldest American to travel in space.
2009	New Ohio Statehouse Museum opens in Columbus.

State motto	"With God, All Things Are Possible"
State capital	Columbus
State flag	The Ohio Burgee
State flower	Red carnation
State bird	Cardinal
State tree	Buckeye
State wildflower	White trillium
Statehood date and number	1803, seventeenth state
State nickname	The Buckeye State or The Mother of Presidents
Total area and U.S. rank	Approximately 41,000 square miles (106,190 sq km); thirty-fourth largest state
Approximate population at most recent census	11,353,140 (2000 census)
Length of coastline	312 miles (502 km)
Highest elevation	Campbell Hill, at 1,549 feet (472 m)
Lowest elevation:	Ohio River, at 455 feet (139 m)

State Flag

State Seal

Major rivers and lakes	Lake Erie, Grand Lake, Ohio River, Cuyahoga River, Miami River, Sandusky River
Hottest temperature recorded	113°F (45°C), near Gallipolis in July 1934
Coldest temperature recorded	-39°F (-39.4°C), in Milligan in February 1899
Origin of state name	Iroquois Indian word meaning "great river"
Chief agricultural products	Corn, soybeans, oats, wheat, sweet corn, tomatoes, cucumbers, grapes, and strawberries; livestock, such as chickens, hogs, and cows; dairy products
Major industries	Manufacturing (steel, automobiles, rubber, chemicals, plastics); mining (coal, natural gas, clay, salt)

State Bird

State Flower

act A bill that has been approved by both the House of Representatives and the Senate.

artifacts Things made, used, and left behind by people.

bill A draft of a law presented to the legislature for a vote.

erode To wear away, such as land.

fertile soil Soil that has many nutrients in it and is good for farming.

glacier A large ice sheet that moves very slowly across an area.

maize Corn cultivated by Native Americans.

manufacturing The process of making a useful product from raw materials.

mammoth An extinct elephant-like animal known for its massive size, large and upwardly curved tusks, and ample body hair; it lived during the prehistoric era.

mastodon An extinct elephant-like animal that was distinguished by its molars with cone-shaped cusps; it lived during the prehistoric era.

prehistoric Before the time of written history.

proclamation A formal public announcement.

till A type of soil characterized by a mixture of clay, silt, and rocks.

Underground Railroad A series of hiding places that slaves in the United States before 1863 used to help them escape to the North or Canada.

Bicycle Museum of America

7 West Monroe Street (St. Rt. 274)

New Bremen, OH 45869

(419) 629-9249

Web site: http://www.bicyclemuseum.com

This museum highlights the history of the bicycle, with more than three hundred bikes permanently on display and rotating exhibits that include Lance Armstrong's Tour de France bike.

International Women's Air & Space Museum

Burke Lakefront Airport, Room 165

1501 North Marginal Road

Cleveland, OH 44114

(216) 623-1111

Web site: http://www.iwasm.org

The International Women's Air and Space Museum preserves the role of women in the history of aviation and space flight.

Ohio Department of Natural Resources

2045 Morse Road, Building C

Columbus, OH 43229-6693

(614) 265-6561

Web site: http://www.dnr.state.oh.us

The Department of Natural Resources oversees Ohio's state parks and recreation areas. It provides information about recycling in Ohio and the state's wildlife, soil, and water resources.

Ohio Historical Society

1982 Velma Avenue

Columbus, OH 43211

(614) 297-2300

Web site: http://www.ohiohistory.org

As one of the largest historical societies in the United States, the Ohio Historical Society preserves the history and archaeology of Ohio, with more than 1.5 million items in its collection.

Rock and Roll Hall of Fame and Museum

1100 Rock and Roll Boulevard

Cleveland, OH 44114

(216) 781-ROCK (7625)

Web site: http://www.rockhall.com

The Rock and Roll Hall of Fame and Museum is dedicated to the history of rock and roll music.

Supreme Court of Ohio

Civic Education Section

65 South Front Street, 1st Floor

Columbus, OH 43215-3431

(614) 387-9223

Web site: http://www.sconet.state.oh.us

The Civic Education Section of Ohio's Supreme Court explains the way the Supreme Court works, and it conducts tours of the court.

Web Sites

Due to the changing nature of Internet links, Rosen Publishing has developed an online list of Web sites related to the subject of this book. This site is updated regularly. Please use this link to access the list:

http://www.rosenlinks.com/uspp/ohpp

Barker, Charles Ferguson. *Under Ohio: The Story of Ohio's Rocks and Fossils*. Athens, OH: Ohio University Press, 2007.

Giblin, James Cross. *The Boy Who Saved Cleveland*. New York, NY: Henry Holt and Co., 2006.

Hart, Joyce. *It's My State!: Ohio*. New York, NY: Marshall Cavendish, Inc., 2006.

Heinrichs, Ann. *Welcome to the U.S.A.: Ohio*. Mankato, MN: The Child's World, 2006.

Jackson, Tom. *The Ohio River* (Rivers of North America). Milwaukee, WI: Gareth Stevens Publishing, 2003.

Reynolds, Cynthia Furlong. *Oliver's Travels: An Ohio Adventure*. Ann Arbor, MI: Mitten Press, 2008.

Roza, Greg. *The Adena, Hopewell, and Fort Ancient of Ohio* (The Library of Native Americans). New York, NY: PowerKids Press, 2005.

Schonberg, Marcia. *Ohio Reader*. Chelsea, MI: Sleeping Bear Press, 2007.

Stille, Darlene. *Ohio*. Danbury, CT: Children's Press, 2008.

Stine, R. L. *It Came from Ohio: My Life as a Writer* (Goosebumps). New York, NY: Scholastic Paperbacks, 1998.

Stine, R. L. *Revenge of the Living Dummy* (Goosebumps). New York, NY: Scholastic Paperbacks, 2008.

BIBLIOGRAPHY

Chemical Heritage Foundation. "Roy J. Plunkett." Retrieved October 20, 2008 (http://www.chemheritage.org/classroom/chemach/plastics/plunkett.html).

Edison Birthplace Association. "Edison Birthplace Museum." Retrieved October 20, 2008 (http://www.tomedison.org).

Estate of Jesse Owens. "Jesse Owens: Track and Field Legend." Retrieved October 20, 2008 (http://www.jesseowens.com/biography).

Legislative Information Systems. "A Brief History of Ohio's State Government." Retrieved October 20, 2008 (http://www.legislature.state.oh.us/about.cfm).

Legislative Information Systems. "The Supreme Court of Ohio." Retrieved October 20, 2008 (http://www.legislature.state.oh.us/judicial.cfm).

NetState. "Introduction to Ohio." Retrieved October 20, 2008 (http://www.netstate.com/states/intro/oh_intro.htm).

Ohio Department of Development. "Economic Overview." August 2008. Retrieved October 20, 2008 (http://www.odod.state.oh.us/research/files/e000.pdf).

Ohio Historical Society. "American Civil War." Retrieved October 20, 2008 (http://www.ohiohistorycentral.org/entry.php?rec = 463).

Ohio Historical Society. "American Frontier." Retrieved October 20, 2008 (http://www.ohiohistorycentral.org/entry.php?rec = 651&nm = american-frontier).

Ohio Historical Society. "American Revolution." Retrieved October 20, 2008 (http://www.ohiohistorycentral.org/entry.php?rec = 464&nm = american-revolution).

Ohio Historical Society. "Appalachian Plateaus." Retrieved October 20, 2008 (http://www.ohiohistorycentral.org/entry.php?rec = 2896&nm = appalachian-plateaus).

Ohio Historical Society. "Black Swamp." Retrieved October 20, 2008 (http://www.ohiohistorycentral.org/entry.php?rec = 654&nm = black-swamp).

Ohio Historical Society. "Camp Sherman." Retrieved October 20, 2008 (http://www.ohiohistorycentral.org/entry.php?rec = 670).

Ohio Historical Society. "French and Indian War." Retrieved October 20, 2008 (http://www.ohiohistorycentral.org/entry.php?rec = 498&nm = french-and-indian-war).

Ohio Historical Society. "Historic Period." Retrieved October 20, 2008 (http://www.ohiohistorycentral.org/entry.php?rec = 1284).

Ohio Historical Society. "Ice Age Ohio." Retrieved October 20, 2008 (http://www.ohiohistorycentral.org/entry.php?rec = 2820&nm = ice-age-ohio).

Ohio Historical Society. "Jack Nicklaus." Retrieved October 20, 2008 (http://www.ohiohistorycentral.org/entry.php?rec = 2152).

Ohio Historical Society. "James M. Spangler." Retrieved October 20, 2008 (http://www. ohiohistorycentral.org/entry.php?rec = 350).

Ohio Historical Society. "Mammal Fossils." Retrieved October 20, 2008 (http://www. ohiohistorycentral.org/entry.php?rec = 1332).

Ohio Historical Society. "Northwest Ordinance." Retrieved October 20, 2008 (http:// www.ohiohistorycentral.org/entry.php?rec = 1747&nm = northwest-ordinance).

Ohio Historical Society. "Ohio General Assembly." Retrieved October 20, 2008 (http:// www.ohiohistorycentral.org/entry.php?rec = 2126&nm = ohio-general-assembly).

Ohio Historical Society. "Ohio Quick Facts." Retrieved October 20, 2008 (http://www. ohiohistorycentral.org/ohio_quick_facts.php).

Ohio Historical Society. "Paleoindian Period." Retrieved October 20, 2008 (http://www. ohiohistorycentral.org/entry.php?rec = 1280).

Ohio Historical Society. "Rankin House." Retrieved October 20, 2008 (http://ohsweb. ohiohistory.org/places/sw14/index.shtml).

Ohio Historical Society. "Vietnam War." Retrieved October 20, 2008 (http://www. ohiohistorycentral.org/entry.php?rec = 1583&nm = vietnam-war).

Ohio Historical Society. "Woodland Period." Retrieved October 20, 2008 (http://www. ohiohistorycentral.org/entry.php?rec = 1279).

Ohio Historical Society. "World War II." Retrieved October 20, 2008 (http://www. ohiohistorycentral.org/entry.php?rec = 1580).

Rock and Roll Hall of Fame and Museum. "Rock and Roll Hall of Fame Press Kit." Retrieved October 20, 2008 (http://www.rockhall.com/images/presskit.pdf).

StateFossils.com. "Ohio State Fossil." Retrieved October 20, 2008 (http://www. statefossils.com/oh/oh.html).

INDEX

About the Author

Kristi Lew is the author of more than two dozen science and social science books for teachers and young people. A former high school science teacher, Lew now makes her living writing nonfiction books, textbook chapters, and magazine articles designed to educate children and adults about science, history, and the environment.

Photo Credits

Cover (top left) Ohio Historical Society; cover (top right) B. Anthony Stewart/National Geographic/Getty Images; cover (bottom), pp. 31, 40 (right) Shutterstock.com; pp. 3, 7, 13, 23, 28, 33, 38 © www.istockphoto.com/Stan Rohrer; p. 4 (top) © GeoAtlas; pp. 6, 39 (left) Courtesy of Robesus, Inc.; p. 8 © Gary Hincks/Photo Researchers, Inc.; p. 10 adapted from Wikimedia Commons; p. 11 © Steve Raymer/Corbis; p. 14 © Marilyn Angel Wynn/Nativestock Pictures/Corbis; p. 17 Library of Congress Geography and Map Division; p. 18 Matthew Brady/Hulton Archive/Getty Images; p. 19 Doreen Spooner/Keystone Features/Hulton Archive/Getty Images; pp. 20, 37 Library of Congress Prints and Photographs Division; p. 22 © Alan Copson/JAI/Corbis; p. 24 © Lee Snider/Photo Images/Corbis; p. 26 Altrendo Travel/Getty Images; p. 29 © Keith Dannemiller/Corbis; p. 30 Andy Sacks/Riser/Getty Images; p. 32 Kenneth Chamberlain, OSU Communications and Technology; p. 34 Alex Wong/Getty Images; p. 35 Brad Barket/Getty Images; p. 40 (left) Wikimedia Commons.

Designer: Les Kanturek; Editor: Andrea Sclarow;
Photo Researcher: Cindy Reiman